Buckminster Fuller to Children of Earth

Text by R. Buckminster Fuller

Compiled and Photographed by Cam Smith

DOUBLEDAY & COMPANY, INC. · GARDEN CITY, NEW YORK · 1972

A portion of the proceeds of this book has been donated to Narconon, a non-profit organization dedicated to reducing crime and drug abuse, for their youth program.

ISBN: 0-385-02979-9
Library of Congress Catalog Card Number 72-86571
Photographs Copyright ©1972 by Cam Smith
Text Copyright© 1972 by R. Buckminster Fuller
All Rights Reserved
Printed in the United States of America
First Edition

Edited by Tom Solari

Sections on pattern integrity and geometry from the film "Buckminster Fuller on Spaceship Earth" used by permission of Robert Snyder

Quotes copyrighted and printed by permission of R. Buckminster Fuller

Cover Design by John Divers

Lithography by Triangle Lithograph · Los Angeles

ENVIRONMENT
to each must be
EVERYTHING
That isn't me

UNIVERSE
in turn must be
ALL THAT ISN'T me
AND me

Buckminster Fuller
March 30 1972

Every time man makes a new experiment he always learns more. He cannot learn less.

I decided that man as
designed was designed to be an extraordinary success;
his characteristics were just magnificent...

...and what would be necessary was really
to find out what were the great comprehensive patterns
operating in Universe.

A child is comprehensive. He wants to understand the whole thing... Universe.

Children will draw pictures with
everything in them... houses and trees and people and
animals... and the sun AND the moon. Grown-up says,
"That's a nice picture, Honey, but you put
the moon and the sun in the sky at the same time
and that isn't right." But the child *is* right!
The sun and moon *are* in the sky at the same time.

A child plays with balls that are round like
the earth and touches whole things. He touches his
mother a lot when he is young...and she
is big and sort of round.
A child thinks in terms of wholes.

A child has 1000 whys...
Why is the sky dark at night?
Why is the earth round?
Why...?

Adults are often busy. They don't answer
the child's questions. And then the child goes to
school and the teacher says,
"First you're going to learn A, B, C."
The child still wants to understand UNIVERSE and
has *big* questions, and the teacher says,
"Never mind that... you learn the parts first... A, B, C..."
Then the child goes to college
and never does get back to the whole.

If you want to do something good for
a child...give him an environment where he can
touch things as much as he wants.

Sometimes we should send people fishing.

I'm not my hair that grows and gets cut off.
I'm not my fingernails. I'm not the food I eat that
turns into cells in my body . . .

Man is a pattern integrity.
He is like the knot tied in a rope.
He is not the rope.
I'm going to splice a piece of manilla rope to
a piece of cotton rope and then splice the
other end of the cotton rope to a piece of nylon rope.
I'm going to make the very simplest
knot that I know. The rope has not done this,
I have done it to the rope.
I can slide this knot along ... I slide it along the
rope and now it leaves the manilla
and now it's on the cotton. I keep sliding it
along and now it's on the nylon.
So ... and suddenly it's off the end.
We say the knot was a pattern integrity, it wasn't
manilla, it wasn't cotton, it wasn't nylon.
Cotton and nylon and manilla;
any one of them are good to let us know
about its shape, what its pattern was,
but it was not that; it had an integrity in its own.

Man sometimes thinks like a tree...
but he was built to move.

All anywhere about man,
within and without,
is eternally, ceaselessly motion,
whether he senses it or not.

Nature is so beautiful...How she is working is so beautiful.

We need to find out what nature is doing so we can be in harmony with her.

The kinds of ways in which man is measuring tend to be much more complicated than what nature is doing. Man starts off teaching his children about measuring with a plane and a line and a pair of lines parallel to each other, and then 90 degrees to that, another pair of lines, making something called a square. But I find that that's all very well if you could really live in a plane; and nobody can live in a plane. Nobody can squash their body into a flat plane. That's not the way nature is. She's not in a plane. She's omni-directional. So when I really look at a square I find it's very unstable. It doesn't want to stay square at all.

We take a side out of the square and...
suddenly it's very stable. It doesn't get all
flexible the way it had been with the square. So this
is what we call tri-angle, three angles.
And triangle, with its three angles,
is the only stable structure.

Nature is doing things in very logical clean-cut
ways. And we begin to study these even more
and I find that she's using beautiful geometry; this
always finally gets down to the simplest geometry
you can get down to. You can't have a
geometrical form of less than four faces: 1, 2, 3, 4.
This is the tetrahedron, four faces,
and then sometime after, it gets its corners knocked
off and it gets to be a *beautiful* tetrahedron.
So this rock was once a tetrahedron.

I begin to look at all these rocks,
and it doesn't look like anything. Then I begin to
pick them up, and I pick up any rock, and
I find it has a beautiful face here, and then
another beautiful face, another
beautiful face...These are not carelessly done.
You begin to study these rocks a little
more, and you find face, face, face, face.
Their corners have been very knocked off...but all
of these rocks were once tetrahedrons.

We find nature doing more with less.
Nature doesn't build things that fall down.

The most creative woodworking I know of is a tree. It can grow its branches straight out... and each limb can support tons of weight.

We should do things with wood that the wood likes. There are certain things
it likes to be used for. When I use wood I make sure it likes what I'm doing to it.

I'm not trying to imitate nature,
I'm trying to find the principles she's using.

Nature has no "weeks." There is no "Monday," "Tuesday," "Friday" in nature.

Energies are not lost ... the universe is not running down.

We say sunset . . . but there is no sunset . . . if you back up and look at earth you see the earth turns.

People sometimes say, "I wonder how it feels to be on a spaceship"... and I say, "Well look around you... you are on one. How does it feel? You are on spaceship Earth."

We are just about
to step out from amongst the pieces of our
just-one-second-ago-broken eggshell.